A FEW
ENCOURAGING
WORDS

A FEW ENCOURAGING WORDS

GLENN DROMGOOLE

ISBN: 979-8-9873351-7-8

Published by Texas Star Trading Company
174 Cypress Street, Abilene, Texas
www.TexasStarTrading.com
(325) 672-9696

Design by Lauren Monsey, Monsey Creative LLC

Printed in the USA

My cup overflows

with beauty I cannot describe

and grace I do not deserve

GLENN DROMGOOLE

Contents

Introduction

A few encouraging words.

Amid the clamor of strident voices and disturbing conflicts, surely we could profit from a few moments of quiet reflection and optimism – whatever our age or station in life.

I hope that one or more of the gentle exhortations in this slender volume will soothe your spirit, enlighten your journey, or provide a respite of peace and grace.

GLENN DROMGOOLE
Abilene, Texas

The High Road

When we reflect on choices made
and routes taken,
we respect ourselves most
for those times when we took
the high road, not the shortcut.

More Civility, Please

The world needs more Civility Champions in our communities, our homes, our workplaces, our politics, our churches.

People who treat everyone with a little more respect.

Who try to find some common ground with those with whom they disagree.

Who consider the possibility at any given time that "I could be wrong."

Who look for an opportunity to make a small difference for good every day.

Who go out of their way to praise exceptional service.

Who teach their children to say "please" and "thank you."

Who practice the "please" and "thank you" rule themselves.

Who make their home a place of acceptance and openness.

Who display good manners as a way of respecting others.

Who embrace good sportsmanship and encourage their children to.

Who advocate for reason.

Who walk through life with a thankful spirit.

Who count their blessings, then count them again.

Who reject the ravings of those with simplistic solutions to complex problems.

Who practice their religion rather than argue it.

Who are easy to get along with.

Who believe in the future and work to make it better.

Who slow down and take time to be more courteous.

Who take the high road.

Civility Champions make their corner of the world a better place.

More civility, please!

A Long-Stemmed Rose

We don't have to do great things to make a difference. Each of us is capable of performing little acts of kindness in whatever we do.

A woman told me this story.

It was Super Bowl Sunday. The woman, a grandmother of seven, was grocery shopping. She had made her way to the checkout line. Three or four other shoppers with full baskets were ahead of her, and there was a little space between them and her.

A young man – she figures he must have been 17 or 18 – suddenly cut in the opening in front of her. When he realized what he had done, he apologized and started to move to the rear of the line.

"Since he had only a long-stemmed rose and I had a full basket of groceries," she said, "at my insistence he remained in line.

"We talked about the Super Bowl game. I commented that he must have someone very special to buy her a long-stemmed rose. He assured me that he did."

When the young man got to the checkout counter, he told the checker to charge him for two roses and he would go get another one. Then he turned and handed the woman behind him the rose and thanked her for letting him break in line.

"I was speechless," she said. "I thanked him and assured him he had made my day, as I was feeling low and alone on that Sunday."

She didn't get the young man's name, but she never forgot his thoughtfulness.

"I hope he received as much pleasure in giving as I did in receiving the beautiful red rose."

The Power of a Smile

Give the World a Smile

It's something anyone can do,
an adult or a child.
We all have it in our power
to give the world a smile.

Smiles Matter

You think that smiles
aren't important?
Just try living
a day without them

Think a Billboard Thought

For billboards to be effective, they need to have a simple message stated in a few words.

What is your billboard thought? If you could proclaim your message to the world in seven words or less, what would you say? It's a good way to evaluate your own priorities as well as your outlook on life.

What is your message? Is your billboard positive or cynical? Does it raise others up or put them down?

The philosopher Aldous Huxley said that after spending his entire lifetime pondering the human condition, the most profound thought he could pass on could be summarized in six words.

His billboard thought: "Try to be a little kinder."

I expressed my own billboard thought as the title of one of my books: "More Civility, Please."

Jesus's billboard thought: "Love God. Love your neighbor."

St. Paul's billboard thought: "And the greatest of these is love."

What's yours?

Loving You!

A Litany for Lovers

Loving you is easy because you make it easy!
Loving you is the best thing I've ever known!
Loving you. Oh, yes!
Loving you. Oh, my!
Loving you. Wow!
Loving you with all my heart!
Loving you with all my life!
Loving you the first thing every morning!
Loving you the last thing every evening!
Loving you all day!
Loving you today, tomorrow, next week, next year.
Loving you always!
Loving you every time I think of you!
Loving you now!
Loving you then!
Loving you forever!

Loving you more!

Loving you more than anything!

Loving you – and thanking you for loving me!

Loving you loving me!

Loving you makes life worth living!

Loving you makes my life complete!

Loving you is comfortable!

Loving you is exciting!

Loving you is fun!

Loving you is an adventure!

Loving you is poetry!

Loving you is a song I haven't written – yet!

Loving you is life!

Loving you is joy!

Loving you is a gift!

Loving you makes all the difference!

Loving you is laughing with you!

Loving you is sharing with you!

Loving you is being with you!

Loving you is going out with you!

Loving you is coming home with you!
Loving you is cooking for you!
Loving you when you cook for me!
Loving you as my partner!
Loving you as my best friend!
Loving you is being your best friend!
Loving you how it began!
Loving you until the end!
Loving you is everything in between!
Loving you is, after all, why we're here!
Loving you, I'll never run out of words!
Loving you, I'll never run out of exclamation marks!
Loving you the rest of our lives!
Loving you right now!
Loving you is simply saying, "I love you!"
I love loving you!
I love you!

The One-Minute Graduation Speech

Graduates, families, and everyone else:

First off, I want to follow the two rules of graduation speeches. The first rule is: Keep It Short. The second rule is: Keep It Short.

So here's what I have to say – in one sentence, seventeen words – describing what I consider a good working philosophy for life. A mission statement, perhaps. At least something worth striving for.

It is this:

Wherever I am, I can do something to make my corner of the world a better place.

Wherever *I am*, I can do something to make my corner of the world a better place.

Wherever I am, I can do *something* to make *my* corner of the world a better place.

I hope that wherever you go, whatever you do, whatever situation you find yourself in, you will try to make your corner of the world a better place.

Be kind. Be generous. Be compassionate. Be honest. Be reasonable. Be thankful. Make a difference with your life.

Make a Difference with Your Life

Whether you are just starting out or seeking a fresh start, you have the opportunity to make this a little better world. Here are ten simple ways to make a difference with your life.

1. Be kind.

Make the effort to do one little act of kindness a day. Encourage others. Praise them. Be polite. Offer to help.

2. Be generous.

Discover that the joy of giving is truly the joy of living. Give compliments. Give time. Give your talent. Give money. Give your best. Give credit to others. Give thanks.

3. Be optimistic.

Optimists see the opportunities and the possibilities in life, not just the problems.

4. Be a doer.

Look for ways to make things better. Suggest solutions. Offer ideas. Don't fall into the trap of complaining about every little thing. Be a doer, not a whiner.

5. Be a communicator.

Develop the ability to communicate one on one. Listen. Smile. Be open to others' ideas. Look for ways to bring people together. Be true to your word.

6. Be a participant.

Take an interest in what is going on in the workplace, the community, the world. Vote. Volunteer. Contribute. Care.

7. Be compassionate.

You have a heart. Listen to it. Be sensitive to those in need. Help when you can. Treat people in need the way you would want to be treated if you were in desperate circumstances.

8. Be reasonable.

Few things are black and white. Look for the shades of gray. Be respectful to those with whom you disagree. Be fair.

9. Be curious.

Be open to new experiences, ideas, people, places. Develop new interests. Be passionate about life. Don't be afraid of change.

10. Be thankful.

Approach life with a thankful spirit, a grateful heart, a joyful outlook. We have benefited from someone else's time, interest, money, encouragement, discipline. Never take these gifts for granted.

In the Spirit

A spiritual life,
it's been shown
throughout time,
doesn't require tomes
of a doctrinal plan.

It's simply trying
in all things
to be kind,
and doing for others
whatever we can.

Five Words of Faith

I believe the Christian faith might well be summed up in the words of five familiar hymns:

"Jesus loves me, this I know."

"Amazing grace, how sweet the sound that saved a wretch like me."

"Count your many blessings, name them one by one."

"Joy to the world."

"Brighten the corner where you are."

Love.

Grace.

Gratitude.

Joy.

Service.

Five words of faith to live by.

We're Not Computers

Computers can do amazing things. They have incredible memories. They can store millions of facts, figures, and names in their "brain."

But, you know, a computer can't appreciate the beauty of a sunset.

It can't know the joy of hearing a newborn baby's first sound.

It can't experience the excitement of catching a fish or hitting a home run.

It can't take pride in watching a child walk across the stage and receive a diploma.

As great as its capacity for memory might be, it can't remember a mother's love or a grandmother's hug or a wife's caress.

It can't know a father's courage or a brother's character or a sister's loyalty.

It can't measure the depth of a friendship.

A computer may be a smart machine, but it can't be as wise as a good teacher.

It can't hope for a better tomorrow.

It can't believe in anything.

It can't know pain or failure or disappointment, but neither can it know elation or satisfaction or contentment or happiness.

A computer can't feel. It can't care. It can't be generous.

We can, and that's the difference.

What's Your Net Worth?

I stared at the question on the form. It asked simply: What is your net worth?

Well, I had never stopped to figure it. What's my net worth? Not much, I imagine. Maybe, if I'm lucky, it comes out a little above zero.

But as I gave the question more thought, I realized I couldn't possibly answer it. Could you?

Net worth is measured in dollars, but real worth can't be counted that way.

How much is a loving husband or wife/companion/best friend worth?

How about your children or grandchildren? How much are they worth? (On a good day.)

Aren't your memories worth something?

What would you give for the experiences you've had?

Who can put a price tag on friendships?

How much would you take for your freedom?

I had the kindest mother anyone could ever have. How much has that been worth over the years?

Laughter is free but invaluable. What's the net worth of a sense of humor?

Principles certainly count for something. But how can they be measured in dollars?

What would you take for your self-respect, your conscience, your integrity? Are they for sale?

The value of an education is much greater than its cost. But how much?

Life itself is the ultimate treasure. Can you place a value on it?

Most of what is important in our lives cannot be bought or sold. It has *value*, to be sure, but not *monetary* value. It can't be measured; it can't be counted. But it is what makes life truly rich.

We're all a lot richer than we think, aren't we, when we stop and add up our true net worth.

I Have Been Diagnosed with a Fatal Disease

I have been diagnosed with a fatal disease.
Everyone who gets this disease eventually dies.

I don't know how long I have, but I think
I should try to make the most of every day.

Come to terms with what is ultimately important.
Spend more time with those I love.

Take more time to appreciate every breath,
every sunrise, every kiss, every smile, every word.

Worry less and enjoy more.
Make my corner of the world a little better place.

For, after all, I don't know how much longer
I will be around.

I have been diagnosed with a fatal disease.
It's called life – and there is no cure.

Gifts We Take for Granted

The Gift of Life – full of possibilities.

The Gift of Time – ours to use wisely.

The Gift of Laughter – the language of joy.

The Gift of Talent – little things we do well.

The Gift of Work – making a difference.

The Gift of Generosity – giving what we can.

The Gift of Kindness – in word and deed.

The Gift of Praise – opening our hearts.

The Gift of Peace – with ourselves and others.

The Gift of Forgiveness – given or received.

The Gift of Sacrifice – unselfishness in action.

The Gift of Gratitude – a thankful spirit.

The Gift of Faith – something to believe in.

The Gift of Hope – anticipating the future.

The Gift of Love – the greatest of them all.

You Just Won the Lottery!

When you think about it, in many ways we've already won the biggest lottery of them all – the lottery of life.

We won the lottery when we received the gift of life and health.

We won the lottery when we were born into a free country and a good home.

We won the lottery when we received an education that allowed us to read and think and earn a good living.

We won the lottery when we were given so many blessings we often take for granted – plenty to eat, a comfortable home, a little money in the bank.

Millions of people around the world – people in this country and right in our own community – would be delighted to trade places with us, for we are truly lottery winners.

A Prayer for Patience

Dear God,
Give me more patience.
Right now!
Amen.

Jesus Haiku

Simple thoughts expressed in 17
syllables, three lines, in a 5-7-5 format.

"Love your enemies!"
Oh, Jesus, why'd you say that?
So, who can we hate?

    "Neighbor as thyself:"
    accept and love who we are,
    and then pass it on.

He walked on water
but doesn't require us to –
just be a life raft.

    Walk the extra mile
    isn't so easy to do
    if you don't have shoes.

"Feed my sheep," He said.
"Feed the hungry and the poor,"
He says to his church.

> A positive faith:
> Isn't that what Jesus preached –
> grace, love, joy, hope, life!

We can see Jesus
in a child's smile, a kind word,
a loving spirit.

> That amazing grace
> isn't just a song we sing –
> it's our salvation.

Let us welcome all
who proclaim Jesus as Lord
to the Lord's table.

Theology summed up:
Jesus loves me, this I know;
Bible tells me so.

> Jesus loved Judas
> even though he betrayed Him –
> and us: same reason.

"Blessed are the poor."
So what would He say today
about the homeless?

> "Father, forgive them."
> He could say that while dying;
> can we, while living?

"Follow me," He said,
not just when it's popular –
but when it is right.

God so loved the world
He sent his son to save it,
not to condemn it.

> The Lord is my rock,
> and the Lord is my shepherd –
> faithful and loving.

Father in heaven –
praise you, thank you, protect us,
forgive us. Amen.

> Two thousand plus years
> and still nothing can compare
> with the truths He taught.

It comes down to this:
in the end, love conquers hate –
can we find a way?

An Attitude of Gratitude

An Attitude of Gratitude is an approach to life that makes life itself more enjoyable – for us and everyone we touch.

Being helpful rather than critical.

Seeing the possibilities rather than the objections.

Seeking out the joy in life and embracing it.

Accepting the imperfections in others the way we hope they accept ours.

Finding time for a smile, a warm thank you, a phone call, a note, a touch, a hug, a handshake.

Believing there is so much to be positive about.

Understanding that life is to be enjoyed, celebrated, lived, shared, loved, given.

Feeling good about ourselves and about others.

Appreciating the things we have rather than taking them for granted.

Hoping for the best and expecting it, from ourselves, from others, from the future.

Reaching out with a helping hand because we were helped when we were helpless.

An Attitude of Gratitude could change our lives if we gave it a chance. It could change our world.

Time to Waste

A few spare moments
with nothing to do
and no place to be
and no one talking
no music playing
nowhere to rush to
just sit and reflect
on the gentle gift
of a little time
preciously wasted.

A Poem to the World

An old man, sitting on the shore,
gazing past the ships at sea,
pondering what might have been,
wishing how the world should be.

His body bears the scars received
from two wars that he believed
would change the world and make it safe;
but now he feels he was deceived.

And why was he the one so spared,
blessed with children and a wife,
while others never had a prayer
to carry out their dreams in life?

Brave men, no doubt, patriots too,
dressed in brown and gray and blue,
sent to kill year after year
for reasons not exactly clear.

And those who died from senseless crimes
during this, the best of times,
passion, anger, greed, and grime,
victims cut short in their prime,

Now as he gazes from the shore,
he imagines he can see
an isle, far on the horizon,
people striving to be free

Of meanness and hostility
hatred, animosity,
people coming to this isle
to talk together for a while.

People from all breeds and clans,
faiths and nations and domains,
it must stop here, it must stop now,
is their common new refrain.

With one accord they do proclaim,
no more carnage, wasted might,
sending children out to fight,
while mothers cry into the night.

So on this isle of sanity,
far from war's profanity,
they offer words of hope and cheer,
kindness and humanity.

They say the generation next
has to find a way to cope,
forgive, not hate, must be the text,
reason, mercy, joy, and hope.

The old man, sitting on the shore,
gazes past the ships at sea,
prays that here forevermore
an old man's vision comes to be.

Work, Work, Work, Work

We love to work.
We hate to work.
We work to put money in our pockets.
We work to put meaning in our lives.
We work to support our families.
We work to support our egos.
We work at home.
We work to get away from home.
We work hard.
We work harder.
We work hardest.
We work hardly.
We work to get ahead.
We work to get by.
We work to stay put.
We work to move on.
We work to accomplish something.

We work to get credit.
We work to make a difference.
We work to eat.
We work to learn.
We work to be with people.
We work in spite of people.
We work out.
We work around.
We work until.
We work toward.
We work on.
We work up.
We work to be satisfied.
We work to satisfy someone else.
We work to succeed.
We work to hang on.
We work to earn a living.
We work to get on with living.
We work to earn a rest.

We work while we're resting.
We work too much.
We work too long.
We work too little.
We work for fun.
We work to pay the bills.
We work to be respectable.
We work to be responsible.
We work to be rewarded.
We work together.
We work in teams.
We work alone.
We work for them.
We work for us.
We work because we have to.
We work because we want to.
We work because we ought to.
We work because we need to.
We work just because.

Seven Wonders

The wonder of today.
The wonder of life.
The wonder of beauty.
The wonder of nature.
The wonder of joy.
The wonder of love.
The wonder of you.

Words of Wisdom

A few that have been especially meaningful to me

Whatever is true, whatever is honorable,
whatever is just, whatever is pure,
whatever is lovely, whatever is gracious—
if there is any excellence, if there is anything worthy
of praise—think about these things.

Philippians 4:8 RSV

The fruit of the Spirit is love, joy, peace,
patience, kindness, goodness,
faithfulness, gentleness, self-control.

Galatians 5:22-23 RSV

One is not born into the world to do everything,
but to do something.

Henry David Thoreau

God gave you a gift of 86,400 seconds today.
Have you used one to say "thank you"?

William Arthur Ward

Three things in human life are important:
The first is to be kind.
The second is to be kind.
And the third is to be kind.

Henry James

The real issue in life is not how many blessings we have,
but what we do with our blessings.
Some people have many blessings and hoard them.
Some have few and give everything away.

Fred Rogers

A happy life is made up of little things
in which smiles and small favors
are given habitually.
A gift sent, a letter written, a call made,

a recommendation given, transportation provided,
a cake made, a book lent, a check sent –
things which are done without hesitation.

Carl Holmes

This was the signature benediction of my friend,
the Rev. Dr. John Claypool (1930-2005),
an influential Baptist and Episcopal
preacher, theologian, and author.

Depart now, in the fellowship of God the Father,
and as you go, remember:
In the goodness of God you were born into this world.
By the grace of God you have been kept,
all the day long, even until this hour.
And by the love of God,
fully revealed in the face of Jesus,
you are being *redeemed*.

We Have the Power

We don't have control over a lot of things in our lives. But it's easy to let that be an excuse for not using all the power we do have.

We have the power to smile.

We have the power to be kind.

We have the power to be courteous and pleasant.

We have the power to praise.

We have the power to offer a compliment.

We have the power to listen.

We have the power to encourage.

We have the power to make others feel important.

We have the power to try.

We have the power to care.

We have the power to do our best.

We have the power to be truthful and honest.

We have the power to participate.

We have the power to give.

We have the power to vote.

We have the power to be optimistic.

We have the power to be happy.

We have the power to treat others with respect.

We have the power to make a difference.

We do not lack for power. We just need to recognize what we have and make the best use of it.

Aha!

Most of our days,
most of our years,
most of our lives
are punctuated
with periods, commas,
colons, semicolons,
and question marks.

But when we look back,
we cherish those
special moments
when the only
appropriate response
was, without question,
an exclamation point!

A Blessing

May your days be filled with beauty,
your hours with joy,
your moments with peace,
and your life with grace.

About the Author

Glenn Dromgoole is the author of more than thirty books. He is a member of the Texas Literary Hall of Fame and was named Abilene's Citizen of the Year in 2013. He and his wife Carol founded Texas Star Trading Company, an independent book and gift store, in 2004.

www.ingramcontent.com/pod-product-compliance
Lightning Source LLC
Chambersburg PA
CBHW061407140726
47997CB00003B/1399